TULIPS

ANN BONAR

A GUIDE TO CULTIVATION

PAVILION

First published in Great Britain in 1993 by
PAVILION BOOKS LIMITED
196 Shaftesbury Avenue, London WC2H 8JL

Concept, design & editorial direction Simon Jennings.
Produced, edited, and designed by Inklink,
Greenwich, London, England.

Text by Ann Bonar
Designed by Simon Jennings & Alan Marshall
Edited by Peter Leek
Instructional illustrations by Robin Harris
Botanical illustrations by Julia Cobbold

First published in The United States of America
by Running Press, Philadelphia, Pennsylvania

Text setting and computer make-up by Inklink, London.
Image generation by Blackheath Publishing Services, London.
Printed in Hong Kong.

A CIP catalogue record for this book is
available from the British Library.

ISBN 1 85793 0525

2 4 6 8 10 9 7 5 3 1

This book may be ordered by post direct from the publisher.
Please contact the Marketing Department.
But try your bookshop first.

TULIPS

A GUIDE TO CULTIVATION
ARRANGED IN THREE CHAPTERS

CONTENTS

THE TULIP
Emblem of perfect love
*"When a young man presents a tulip to
his mistress he gives her to understand,
by the general colour of the flower,
that he is on fire with her beauty, and by
the black base of it his heart is
burnt to a coal."*
SIR JOHN CHARDIN, TRAVELS IN PERSIA, 1686

INTRODUCTION

MOST GARDENS INCLUDE TULIPS – even if only a few small clumps that have grown in the same place for years, providing a splash of colour in late spring.

But tulips can be much more exciting than that. Today, there are all sorts of flower shapes, colours, and plant heights. There are now even scented tulips, and tulips that have variegated leaves with cream or white markings. And if you choose appropriate varieties, you can have tulips flowering in your garden continuously from early spring into early summer.

Because there are so many different kinds, tulips can be grown in a variety of situations – including herbaceous borders, rock gardens, rose beds, grassy slopes, pool-sides, containers, and between paving on patios. Indeed, tulips are the most versatile of flowers, and their vivid colours combine superbly with all kinds of garden plants.

The first section of this book deals with the long and fascinating history of tulip growing, starting with the Turks, who were the major tulip gardeners for 150 years, until the Dutch became infected with "tulipomania" in the seventeenth century. Holland is now generally regarded as the home of the tulip, and it was Dutch settlers and traders that were responsible for tulips spreading to many parts of the world.

The second section of the book is concerned with the different types and classes of tulips, such as lily-flowered, fringed, and multifloras, with examples of named varieties that are interesting to grow.

The last section provides information and advice on growing tulips: how to plant them, the kind of soil in which they grow best, lifting and storing, increasing, forcing, pests and diseases – in fact, all you need to know in order to grow healthy, long-lived plants.

CHAPTER

I

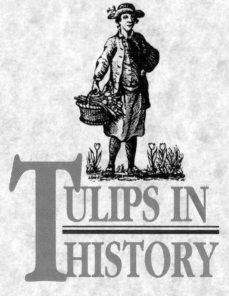

TULIPS IN HISTORY

NOT ONE OF FLORA'S BRILLIANT RACE
A FORM MORE PERFECT CAN DISPLAY;
ART COULD NOT FEIGN MORE SIMPLE GRACE
NOR NATURE TAKE A LINE AWAY.

FROM "ON PLANTING A TULIP-ROOT"
JAMES MONTGOMERY 1771-1854

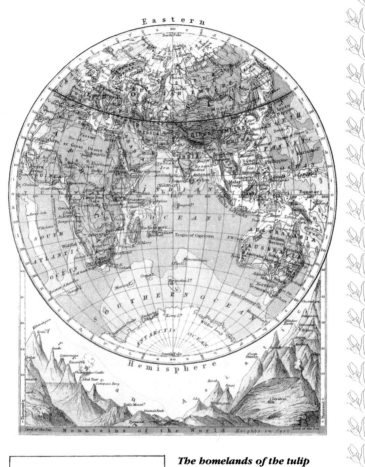

Botany

The homelands of the tulip
The natural habitat of most of the "parent species" from which modern garden tulips are derived is a corridor of land that follows the 40th parallel, extending from the Mediterranean to China, taking in Asia Minor, Turkestan, and the Caucasus on the way. The tulip is amazingly versatile. Many species originate in countries where summers are baking hot, following warm showery springs; in mountainous areas, the bulbs bury themselves deeply to avoid damage from wind, ice, and snow.

ORIGINS OF THE TULIP

"GRIFFINS AND UNICORNS might just as well have been the subjects of speculation." This terse comment, made by a writer in 1897, was his verdict on an extraordinary epidemic of gardening madness that gripped Holland for three years during the seventeenth century and which came to be known as tulipomania.

However, before events reached the extreme heights of what was to all intents and purposes a form of gambling, the tulip had already enjoyed considerable popularity in the sixteenth century as it spread from Turkey through Europe into Britain. From Europe, the bulbs were eventually taken across the Atlantic to America.

The tulip is mainly a plant of the Mediterranean region and central Asia, but Turkey in particular is the home of many species and it was in this country that the first garden varieties appeared. Curiously for such a widespread genus, there is no record of its being much cultivated before the sixteenth century apart from a few vague and somewhat unsubstantial references.

In an illuminated Bible of the twelfth century, some of the flowers decorating the capital letters have been identified as tulips. As to firsthand accounts, some time between 1546 and 1549 a French traveller named Pierre Belon reported that "red lilies" were to be found in every Turkish garden. Since the Turks had a marked preference for tulip varieties with pointed lily-like petals, it seems highly likely that these "lilies" were in fact tulips.

11

Stolen seeds

In 1554 an Austrian diplomat named Ogier Ghiselin de Busbecq, representing the Emperor Ferdinand I at the court of Suleiman the Magnificent (1494-1566) in Turkey, recorded in letters to his friends at home his enthusiasm for a flower new to him, much grown in Turkey, and not previously seen in Europe.

There was, he wrote, "an abundance of flowers everywhere ... and those which the Turks called *tulipam*, much to our astonishment because it was almost midwinter, a season unfriendly to flowers .... The *tulipam* however have little or no smell but are much admired for the beauty and variety of their colours."

One of Busbecq's friends was Carolus Clusius, who became Professor of Botany at Leiden University, in Holland, and established the botanic garden there that still exists today. Busbecq sent Clusius some tulip seeds and bulbs, which he grew in Vienna before moving to Holland. Among them was the first double flower – "a bad green," though a red and a yellow soon followed.

Clusius went on to grow tulips successfully in Leiden, in 1593. When asked to sell them, he named a price too high for anyone even to consider, as he did not want to part with them. As a result, most of the best of his tulips were stolen one night, and the seeds derived from them sold throughout Holland by the thieves.

The earliest known European illustration of a tulip is in a book published in 1561, drawn by the Swiss botanist Conrad von Gesner, who saw tulips growing in a garden at Augsburg in 1559. But in Turkey tulips had been assiduously cultivated for some time. Suleiman had even made it the official flower of his court, and grew tulips throughout the extensive royal gardens. Tulips were called *lalé* by the Turks – the name tulip was mistakenly acquired through Busbecq's interpreter, who gave him the word for turban (*tulbënd* in Turkish, which became *tulipa* in medieval Latin).

From the Orient to the Occident

During the reign of Suleiman the Magnificent the tulip was declared the official flower of the Turkish court. From Turkey, it was introduced into Europe by the Austrian diplomat Busbecq. The diplomat sent some seeds home to his friend the botanist Clusius in Vienna, who successfully cultivated them.

‡ *Tulipa ſerotina polyclados major flo.flaͳͤ fundo nigro,* Cluſij.
Cluſⷨⷨ his greater many branched Tulip with a yellow floure, and blacke bottome.

SULEIMAN THE MAGNIFICENT

OGIER GHISELIN DE BUSBECQ

Early illustrations

The earliest known European tulip illustration appeared in 1561. As this new flowering plant became more widely known, it provided a superb subject for botanical illustrators. The example above is of a T. CLUSIANA from Gerard's HERBALL of 1597.

CAROLUS CLUSIUS

Strange foreign flowers

In Britain the tulip seems to have arrived in 1578, as witness an account by Richard Hakluyt written in 1582: "Within these foure yeares there have been brought into England from Vienna in Austria, divers kinds of flowers called Tulipas."

By 1597 the herbalist John Gerard was writing that the "Tulipa or the Dalmation Cap is a strange and forrein floure" and that a friend of his, James Garret, had been growing them for twenty years. Gerard also makes one of the very few references to eating tulip bulbs, observing that "the roots preserved with sugar, or otherwise dressed, may be eaten, and are not unpleasant nor any way offensive meat, but rather good and nourishing." Indeed, in modern times their nutritional value came to the rescue of starving Dutch families when food was scarce during the Second World War.

John Parkinson, writing about thirty years after Gerard, describes over 150 varieties in his *Paradisi in Sole Paradisus Terrestris* – such as *Testamentum Brancion*, "a faire deepe red or lesse red with a pale yellow or butter coloured edge." Another thirty years on, John Rea, in his *Flora Ceres et Pomona*, listed 174 varieties, mentioned that there were yet more, and divided them into three groups – *Praecoses*, *Medias*, and *Serotinas* ("earlies," "midseasons," and "lates") – and this grouping has continued to the present day. Rea described a tulip flower as being "in fashion like unto a lily composed of six leaves, green at the first and closed, which warmed by the

Knight of ye golden tulip

14

PL. XVIII

To the Rt. Honble. the Earl of Suffolk
This Plate is most humbly Dedicated by his Lordships most Obedt. Servt.
Moses Harris

sun open and change into several glorious divers colours variously mixed, edged, striped, feathered, garded, agotted, marbled, flaked or speckled, even to admiration."

At this time also, John Tradescant, gardener to Charles I of England, was growing fifty different varieties in his own garden. Some years later, General Lambert, a Roundhead commander, was known as "Lambert, Knight of ye Golden Tulip," and in a pack of satirical playing cards issued by the Royalists he was shown cultivating tulips in his garden in Wimbledon.

TULIPOMANIA

BUT IT WAS IN HOLLAND in the seventeenth century that tulips became a national cult, almost a disease. To some extent it was a case of outdoing the neighbors, since the wealthy were easily tempted by such highly visible status symbols. The most sought-after bulbs were the "broken varieties," later called Rembrandts. These are the beautiful tulips with flaming and feathering, contrasting with the base colour, that figure so prominently in the Dutch flower paintings of the time. The fact that this variation in colour is due to a virus infection was not known then, but because of the virus no one could tell how the flower from a new bulb would be coloured or marked.

Because growing tulips was such a gamble and the flowers were so popular, feverish speculation in bulbs became rife. Often the bulbs were sold sight unseen while still in the ground – then sold on again at a profit, and sold and resold over and over again. So irresistible was the desire to own a tulip that would outdo everyone else's in colour, size, and beauty that prices went quite mad and it became possible to make a fortune in a matter of days or weeks. Indeed, if cash was not available to pay for a bulb, goods would be offered – such as a "sideboard of ebony decorated with many mirrors," or a horse and carriage to complete a transaction for five pounds of 'Yellow Crown' tulips (the asking price was 1,875 florins, but the buyer had only 500 florins available).

The most extreme example of all was the selling of one 'Viceroy' bulb for two loads of wheat, four loads of rye, four fat oxen, eight fat pigs, twelve sheep, two barrels of butter, a thousand pounds of cheese, two hogsheads of wine, four barrels of special beer, a silver beaker, a suit of clothes, and a complete bed, the whole being valued at 2,500 florins. Later one bulb of '*Semper Augustus*', a very famous tulip, was sold for nearly 5,000 florins, together with a new carriage and pair.

Tulipomania lasted for three years, from 1634 to 1637. Then suddenly the market crashed, and many buyers and sellers were ruined overnight. The "wind trade," as it came to be known, because the trade in tulips was as unpredictable as the wind, had blown itself out.

Monkey business
A trenchant comment on the whole business was made by Jan Brueghel II (1601-78) with a painting in which monkeys took the place of humans discussing the buying and selling of tulips over the kind of lavish meal generally provided at such transactions.

Turkish tulip festivals

WHILE TULIP FEVER did not seize the rest of Europe to quite the same extent, nevertheless tulips were among the most popular flowers. In Turkey, in particular, they increased steadily in favour throughout the seventeenth century until there was a kind of mild tulipomania early in the 1700s. Their popularity with Turkish royalty resulted in a law that forbade any trade in tulips outside Constantinople, the punishment for any breach of the prohibition being, at the very least, exile.

The Grand Vizier of the time, nicknamed Lalizari ("lover of tulips"), was known to have more than 500,000 tulips in his gardens, where tulip festivals were held at the time of the full moon. One of these festivals was held specially to mark the birth of Mahmud II, in 1783, whose mother was said to be a cousin of the wife of the French emperor Napoleon.

On the occasion of a festival the gardens were exquisitely decorated, and guests were expected to wear colours that blended with those of the flowers. Vases of tulips were placed in an enormous amphitheatre of wooden stands, amongst which were glass globes filled with coloured water, lamps, and cages of canaries and other songbirds. Flowers were laid out on the ground to form patterns like those of carpets, and were further used to make archways, towers, and pyramids.

On one evening a year, at sunset, the gates of the gardens were locked, cannons fired a salute, and the ladies of the harem were allowed into the tulip-bedecked courtyard, which was lit by hundreds of sweet-smelling torches. Acording to one account, as the doors leading to the courtyard were opened, the women would "rush out on all sides, like bees settling on the flowers, and stopping continually on the honey they found there."

A register of tulips called the *Ferahengiz* was kept, in which 1,588 varieties were recorded, and the Grand Vizier published a book of his own that listed more than 1,300. Their names give a good indication of how highly they were regarded: 'Beauty's Reward', 'Lover's Dream', 'Lightning Flash', 'Ruby of Paradise', and 'Pink of Dawn'. Opposite is a description of a perfect tulip of the time.

The chosen of the chosen

"She has the colour of the violet, and the curved form of the new moon. Her markings are rightly placed, clean and well proportioned. Her shape is like the almond, needle-like and ornamented with pleasant rays. Her inner petals are like a well, as they should be; her outer petals a little open, this too as it should be. The white ornamental petals are absolutely perfect. She is the chosen of the chosen."

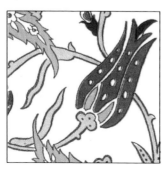

The illustrations show tile designs with tulips from the RUSTEM PASHA MOSQUE in Turkey, built in 1561. Rustem Pasha was Suleiman the Magnificent's son-in-law and one of the richest Ottoman viziers.

19

The tulip in art

Tulips found such universal favour that artists everywhere painted them, sometimes as single flowers and sometimes as floral arrangements, either consisting of tulips alone or a mixture of flowers, as in those glorious oil paintings so characteristic of the time.

Much space was devoted to illustrations of tulips in books, and some exquisite engravings were done, particularly by Crispin van der Passe (b.1589), to illustrate the many, many varieties that were grown. The son of a Dutch family of engravers, van der Passe specialized in copper-plate engravings, which had the advantage of being clear cut and distinct. When only 25 years old, he published a book in two volumes, *Hortus Floridus*, illustrated with some of the best engravings of tulips that have ever been made. He also produced prints that show how tulips were planted and displayed in seventeenth-century Dutch gardens.

Ceramics, ranging from ornaments to tableware, often featured tulips, and some beautiful pieces have survived from this period. with many fine pieces to be seen in Dutch museums. Tiles were frequently decorated with tulips, particularly in Holland, and sixteenth-century tiling from Turkey with a tulip as the centrepiece of each tile clearly shows the Turkish preference for pointed petals and multi-coloured flowers (see page 19). Tulips were also employed for other decorative purposes. In France, ladies at the court of Louis XV used tulips to trim their plunging necklines – the more expensive the better!

It is sometimes the case that a way of life that has been established for years, even centuries, is disrupted by war, never to return. One of the casualties of the French Revolution and Napoleon's invasion of Europe was tulip fever. The long period of war forced entire populations to face the economic realities of life and, while tulips were still popular, they came a long way behind necessities

such as food and warmth. However, gradually a new way of life evolved, and the cultivation and breeding of tulips became established as a commercial enterprise, particularly in Holland and Britain. It became the norm for tulips to be grown in every garden, instead of being largely restricted to Royal gardens and those of the great estates.

21

TULIPS IN THE NEW WORLD

WHEN THEY SET SAIL FOR THE NEW WORLD, English, Dutch, and German settlers took tulip bulbs with them. There are records of tulips being seen growing near the Hudson River and in New Amsterdam; Peter Stuyvesant, the famous Governor of New York, grew them, and there is a portrait of Mrs Wynant van Zandt, probably done in 1725, that gives great prominence to the tulip she is holding.

One unhappy gardener, Thomas Hancock, living in Boston, Massachusetts, wrote a letter to an English nursery in 1737, complaining about some plants they had sent him. None of them, it seems, had grown, and his postscript adds a final plaintive note of disgust: "The Tulip Roots you were pleased to make a present of to me are all Dead as well."

In 1760, a nursery in Boston ran an advertisement in the local paper offering "50 Different Sorts of Mixed Tulip Roots" for sale, and President Jefferson (1743-1826) made notes about his tulips in his famous garden books. He must have been fond of them, since his granddaughter Anne wrote to him when he was away from his garden at Monticello that the tulips were all budding but were not growing "as regularly this spring as they did the last."

George Washington's garden at Mount Vernon has been restored and replanted meticulously, just as it was, using Washington's own garden notes, and tulips form a large part of the spring display. In New York, the garden at the Frick Collection is a re-creation of a French eighteenth-century design featuring tulips, which provides a delightful cool green oasis in a desert of city buildings. The restoration of colonial Williamsburg shows that it had a variety of gardens in the eighteenth century, mostly somewhat formal, in which the tulip was the preferred flower. Its only serious competitors were the clove pink and larkspur, although these, along with roses and hollyhocks, were summer flowers. Dutch and English tulip varieties were grown, often within small, neat box hedges or miniature wicket fences.

The formality of the tulip lent itself ideally to the desire for formal gardens, itself a reaction against the wildness of the untamed countryside surrounding the towns. Their enormous range of colouring, too, made them essential for spring-flowering schemes and ensured a kaleidoscope of colour after the monochromes of winter.

In Independence Park, Philadelphia, an eighteenth-century garden has been made on a small piece of land said to have once been the garden of the colonist William Hamilton. The design and plantings faithfully follow those detailed by the eighteenth-century horticulturist, and every year the Dutch Bulb Institute contributes more than fifty tulip varieties, which make up the main display throughout the garden.

Peter Stuyvesant
1592-1672
The famous Dutch administrator in the New World is known to have grown tulips in New York (New Amsterdam) in the seventeenth century.

Tulip shows & festivals

During the last century tulip exhibitions and festivals began to make their appearance, and these have proliferated steadily to the present day.

North America

One of the biggest tulip festivals is held each spring in Michigan City, Indiana, and several festivals occur annually in the Midwest that are derived from the nineteenth century. In fact, wherever there were Dutch settlers there is now likely to be a tulip festival.

Canada, too, joins in the general enthusiasm, and at the annual spring festival held in Ottawa in May there is what the city claims to be the biggest tulip show in the North American continent.

Britain

In Britain there are tulip fields to rival those of Holland in the flat sandy soil of Lincolnshire, particularly around Spalding. A show garden has been created there, called Springfields, planted with tulips both outdoors, among trees, water, and lawns, and under glass. Each spring there is a tulip show and parade, centred around Springfields, in which floats decorated with tulips travel along a four-mile route presided over by a Tulip Queen and her Court. Extraordinary subjects are modelled in tulip flowers, such as animals and Disney characters.

It may seem wasteful to use flowers to decorate these floats, but they are in fact deliberately cut off as part of the process of bulb production and would otherwise be discarded. Using the flowers to provide beautiful show-pieces for the parades at least allows them to have one brief moment of glory.

Holland & the Keukenhof

Perhaps the most famous show garden associated with tulips is the Keukenhof, in Holland. Originally, the area now occupied by the garden was forest, part of the grounds of a castle that acquired its name through the legendary reputation of the food provided at the banquets held there – *keukenhof* meaning "kitchen yard."

The Keukenhof has a beautiful site containing lakes, large trees, and extensive lawns and streams, interspersed with walks and plantings of tulips, hyacinths, and other spring-flowering bulbs. Summer-flowering plants continue the display, and statues and sculptures of various kinds add to the visual feast. These are changed annually, being obtained afresh each year from different countries.

The tulips are at their best for about six weeks. The display is open from a week before Easter – and even when Easter is early, there's still an incredible display in the glasshouses that form an integral part of the gardens.

DUTCH BULBFIELDS IN FULL BLOOM

TULIPS TODAY

TULIPS CONTINUED TO GAIN IN POPULARITY throughout the nineteenth century in Europe, and also in America. In fact, gardens of the time were often designed and planted with tulips as a main feature – for instance, Biltmore Gardens in North Carolina, which are part of the Vanderbilt estates. Nineteenth-century Dutch settlers took their tulips with them to the Middle West, where they still flourish; and at Sterling Forest Garden, in New York State, there's a living tulip "library" featuring about 140 varieties.

Although the two world wars put a stop to the development of tulips, the hiatus was only temporary. Today, with new mutations and controlled breeding, the tulip continues to gain both in popularity and in beauty. The viridifloras are becoming a distinct group, with green streaking and banding that contrasts with the base colour. Multifloras, which have several blooms to a stem, are another expanding group – and it is probably only a matter of time before scented garden varieties become the norm rather than the exception.

Since the early days, when tulips were grown primarily for garden display, a new trade has grown up – in cut flowers. This is now a massive industry in Holland, a country which is sometimes referred to as the tulip's spiritual home. Indeed, the Dutch are notable for having taken the tulip to their hearts from the earliest beginnings of the tulip trade in the sixteenth century. Nowadays, however, tulips are popular in all countries that have suitable conditions for their cultivation.

Tulip

CHAPTER
II

TULIPS FOR YOUR GARDEN

THE TULIP AND THE BUTTERFLY
APPEAR IN GAYER COATS THAN I
FROM "AGAINST PRIDE IN CLOTHES"
ISAAC WATTS 1674-1748

Tulips for your garden

Despite its relatively short history, the tulip has long been one of the the most popular garden flowers. Many hybrids and sports (mutants) have appeared only to be lost, but the continued proliferation of hybrids, together with the great variability of tulip species in the wild, has led to a multiplicity of colours and flower shapes – and today interesting new forms and colourings are still being evolved. In fact, few garden flowers are so versatile – and few are so easy to grow.

As we have seen, the home of the tulip extends from the Mediterranean region (mainly Spain, Italy, Greece, and Turkey), right across to China, taking in Asia Minor, Turkestan, and the Caucasus on the way. It is frequently found in mountainous terrain, often in places where the summer is baking hot, following warm, showery springs. Winter in such places is often cold enough for snow and ice, but the tulips bury themselves deeply enough to escape being damaged by these conditions.

In their natural surroundings tulip species are often found in varying forms, not quite different enough to be classed as distinct varieties but nevertheless not quite like the true species. This is partly due to cross-fertilization, and partly to soil and weather conditions. Consequently, it is not surprising that modern garden tulips display such diversity, especially as they have been bred continuously for at least four centuries.

In most bulb catalogues tulips are divided into three large groups: early-flowering, midseason, and late-flowering. Within these seasonal groups are flowers of different shapes and heights, single-flowered and double-flowered varieties, and some that have colour-marked leaves. These categories include a number of species tulips that are particularly important for gardening purposes, as well as the varieties derived from them. The other species, which now tend to be listed separately in gardening books and specialist catalogues, are described in the section on species tulips at the end of this chapter.

28

The life cycle of a tulip

Autumn
Roots begin to develop shortly after planting. Leaves and then flowers gradually mature. Buds increase in size and develop fleshy scales until flowering time.

Spring
Leaves appear above ground, followed by flower stems. Inside the scales, flower initials for next year's blooms develop within the main new bulb.

Late spring
The current season's leaves complete their growth, then act as food factories for the developing new bulbs.

Early summer
The old bulb shrivels and the leaves die down.

Mid/late summer
Buds form in the axils of the thickened scales of the offsets. Flower and leaf embryos develop from the spring initials.

Guide to flowering times

EARLY-FLOWERING
(EARLY SPRING TO THE EARLIER PART OF MID SPRING)
Single early hybrids.
Species tulips:
T. fosteriana, T. kaufmanniana.

MIDSEASON
(MID SPRING TO EARLY IN LATE SPRING)
Double-flowered hybrids
("early doubles").
Darwin hybrids
(single-flowered).
Triumph tulips
(hybrids between early-flowering and late-flowering varieties, single-flowered).
Species tulips:
T. greigii.

LATE-FLOWERING
(LATE SPRING INTO EARLY SUMMER)
Darwin & Cottage tulips
(single-flowered).
Lily-flowered
(single-flowered).
Fringed tulips
(single-flowered).
Viridiflora hybrids
(single-flowered).
Rembrandts
(single-flowered, broken colouring).
Parrot hybrids
(single-flowered).
Double late tulips
(peony-flowered).
Multiflora hybrids.

NOTE:
IN BOTANICAL NAMES,
T. = Tulipa.

29

Anatomy of a Tulip

Tulips are bulbous plants, which means they have a swollen fleshy structure beneath the ground from which the flowering stem and leaves emerge. At the base of this fleshy structure there is a roundish flat area from which the roots develop, called the basal plate, which is in fact a drastically truncated stem. The whole is enclosed in a brown papery skin.

1 The tulip bulb

The bulb of the tulip is essentially a bud surrounded by swollen leaf bases that look like fleshy scales. These are swollen because they have become adapted to storing food during the resting period forced on the plant in its native habitat by heat and drought.

At the time of planting, during the later part of the autumn, a tulip bulb consists of the white fleshy scales described above (which do not in fact develop into leaves), surrounding an embryo flower and three to six embryo leaves at the centre of the bulb. There are also minute bud structures present in the axils of the scales.

2 After planting

Once the bulb has been planted, roots grow from the basal plate, and the buds start to develop the scales that will become fleshy storage organs like those of the parent bulb. This process continues throughout the winter, and at the same time the flower and leaf embryos mature and become elongated.

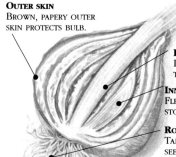

OUTER SKIN
BROWN, PAPERY OUTER SKIN PROTECTS BULB.

FLOWER EMBRYO
DEVELOPS FROM THIS AREA.

INNER SCALES
FLESHY INNER SCALES STORE FOOD.

ROOTS
TAP INTO THE EARTH SEEKING ESSENTIAL NOURISHMENT.

PETALS
DISTINCTIVE COLOURS
ATTRACT POLLINATORS.

STIGMAS
ATTACHED TO
THE STYLE.

STEM
TRANSPORTS FOOD FROM
BULB AND LEAVES TO
WHEREVER IT IS
NEEDED.

SECTION OF TULIP STEM

LEAVES
MANUFACTURE FOOD
FROM THE AIR WHEN
LIGHT IS PRESENT.

3 Springtime

As spring approaches, first the leaves and then the flowering stem emerge above the ground. While this is happening, the flower initials (the microscopic beginnings of the flowers) for next year's blooms form in the centre of the newly thickening scales that developed from the autumn onwards. This season's leaves finish their growth in late spring, then act as food factories for the developing new bulbs. At the same time, the current season's thickened bulb scales release stored nutrients and shrivel away.

4 After flowering

By the time the plants are dug up after flowering, the new bulbs will be fully formed. The central one becomes even more active internally, as the flower embryo and leaf embryos develop from the spring initials, and a new set of buds begins to appear in the axils of the fleshy scales. The bud formed right in the centre of the bulb, close to the flowering stem, produces the main new bulb and the best flower or flowers.

In each bulb there may be an offset from a bud that has developed in the axil of the brown papery outside skin. This offset is called a "maiden," and it produces a single leaf during the summer that helps to feed it. As a result, it flowers almost as well as the main new bulb.

The temperature after the leaves have completely died down is important. It needs to be fairly high to ensure that the flower embryos develop as they should. For about six weeks during mid and late summer it should be about 68-75°F (19-24°C), dropping to the lower level at night and not rising above it – otherwise proper development will not take place. If an abnormal period of cold weather occurs in early autumn, with temperatures around 40°F (4°C), flowering may occur much earlier the following spring than it otherwise would.

EARLY-FLOWERING TULIPS

THIS CATEGORY INCLUDES both species tulips and single-flowered garden tulips. The former are two of the best-known species – *T. fosteriana* and *T. kaufmanniana* and their varieties. They are also two of the prettiest.

Early-flowering species
*T. FOSTERIANA and T. KAUFMANNIANA
and their hybrids are among the
most popular of the early-flowering
tulips. They do well in deep soil, in
a sunny position. The illustration
shows T. FOSTERIANA 'CANTATA' (top)
and T. KAUFMANNIANA 'SHAKESPEARE'
(bottom).*

T. fosteriana

A native of central Asia, particularly the areas around Bukhara and Samarkand, *T. fosteriana* has the largest flowers of any of the species tulips. They are 10in (25cm) wide when fully open and are coloured a brilliant red, with a black basal blotch to each petal. The height is about 12-18in (30-45cm), flowering time early spring. Varieties include 'Orange Emperor' (which is a plain orange colour); 'Sweetheart' (yellow, paling to white on the margins); and 'Tender Beauty' (rose-pink, paling to white in the centre).

T. FOSTERIANA 'ORANGE EMPEROR'

T. kaufmanniana

This is sometimes called the "waterlily tulip," as the pointed white or pale-yellow petals turn back widely in the sun from a flower that is cone-shaped when closed. The height is 4-9in (10-23cm), and it is the first tulip to bloom in early spring. Of the varieties, 'Gluck' is an old favourite, 4in (10cm) tall, with yellow flowers that are edged with red on the outside; it has chocolate-striped leaves. 'Shakespeare', 6in (15cm) high, is a blend of orange and apricot on the outside, with the inside of the petals yellow flushed with red. 'Heart's Delight', 4in (10cm), has pink-and-white petals, with a yellow base, and leaves that are heavily chocolate-marked.

T. KAUFMANNIANA 'GLUCK'

Single early hybrids

The single garden varieties are characterized by flowers that have rounded petal tips and rounded bases. They do well in containers. Delightful examples include 'Apricot Beauty', a blend of rose-pink and apricot, 16in (40cm) tall; 'De Wet', orange overlaid with gold, fragrant, 12in (30cm); and 'Keizerskroon', red with a broad yellow edge, 14in (35cm).

SINGLE EARLY 'APRICOT BEAUTY'

MIDSEASON TULIPS

BY MID SPRING tulips are beginning to get into their stride, although their main flowering season is not until late spring. Midseason tulips include *T. greigii* and hybrids derived from it, double-flowered hybrids, the Darwin hybrids, and the Triumph tulips. As well as being midseason, the last three are midway in height between the early-flowering and late-flowering groups, being about 18in (45cm) tall. All do well in cooler gardens and exposed positions, as they are extremely hardy and strong enough to stand up to high winds.

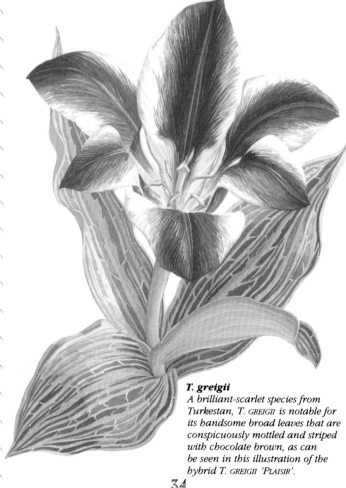

T. greigii
A brilliant-scarlet species from Turkestan, T. GREIGII is notable for its handsome broad leaves that are conspicuously mottled and striped with chocolate brown, as can be seen in this illustration of the hybrid T. GREIGII 'PLAISIR'.

T. greigii hybrids

The outstanding leaf markings of *T. greigii* have been passed on to its garden hybrids, which are 24in (60cm) or so high. 'Plaisir' has red petals with yellow edges and a black-and-yellow base. 'Donna Bella' is a creamy yellow with a black base topped with red; its leaves have striking dark-brown stripes. 'Cape Cod' is yellow with a red streak and red basal blotch. The scarlet flowers of 'Red Riding Hood' contrast dramatically with its brownish-purple leaf markings.

PLAISIR

CAPE COD

RED RIDING HOOD

35

FRINGED BEAUTY

Double-flowered hybrids

The double-flowered midseason tulips are especially attractive, and the modern hybrids have been bred with stems stout enough to carry the heavy heads, which are often as much as 4in (10cm) wide. They are frequently referred to as "early double" tulips, but this simply indicates that they flower earlier than the "late doubles" and does not mean that they flower early in the season. Three that contrast in colour are 'Fringed Beauty', a brilliant-red variety with a finely fringed yellow edge, 12in (30cm); 'Orange Nassau', orange-red, 11in (28cm); 'Peach Blossom', rose-pink and white, (11in) 28cm.

PEACH BLOSSOM

Darwin hybrids

These are similar in shape to the late-flowering Darwin tulips except for the base of the flower, which is square like that of their other parent, *T. fosteriana*.

Pretty ones include 'Daydream', a glowing sunset colour, in shades of yellow and apricot deepening to orange; 'Queen Wilhelmina' is light red, edged finely with orange and marked with yellow at the base of the petals; 'Elizabeth Arden', a variety introduced in 1990, has flowers that are a deep rose-pink striped with an even deeper shade of pink.

ELIZABETH ARDEN

36

Triumph group

The Triumphs acquired their name because they soon proved themselves to be ideal and highly popular garden plants. 'New Design' is a breakaway. It has white flowers edged with pink, a yellow base, and leaves edged with white. 'Attila' is deep purple; 'Bing Crosby' scarlet; 'High Society' is orange, yellow, and salmon. 'Garden Party' is fun: it is a rose-pink cone-shaped tulip with a broad white central triangle on the outside of each petal.

NEW DESIGN

BING CROSBY

CharlesDarwin (1809-82)
Best known for his work THE ORIGIN OF THE SPECIES, *the pioneering naturalist lent his name to the Darwin and Darwin-hybrid tulip groups (see pages 36 and 38).*

GARDEN PARTY

37

LATE-FLOWERING TULIPS

THIS CATEGORY CONTAINS THE MAJORITY of the garden tulips, the biggest group of which consists of the Darwins, under whose umbrella the Cottage tulips are now included. They have single flowers that are globular in shape, with rounded petal tips. The Darwins were named for Charles Darwin, as they were introduced soon after he died, the first ones being bred in 1889 by Jules Lenglart of Lille, who used Breeder tulips (see page 44) as parents for many of them. The average height ranges from 24 to 28in   (60 to 70cm).

Darwins

'Clara Butt' is a reliable favourite among the Darwins; it bears soft-pink flowers on particularly strong stems and always makes a good show. 'Black Swan' is a purple shade of black; in complete contrast, 'Snowpeak' is pure white, while 'Shirley' is white delicately edged with purple. 'Sweet Harmony' is yellow, changing to cream at the top of the petals.

The Darwin group
These are the longest-lasting of all tulips and make excellent cut flowers. This group contains the greatest number of cultiv-ated varieties and they are usually of a single colour. The illustration shows 'ABE LENSTRA' (top) and 'QUEEN OF NIGHT' (bottom).

Cottage tulips

These are a rather amorphous mixture of garden varieties that were grown in cottage gardens from the seventeenth century, and until recently they were treated as a distinct class. In effect, they consist of those types that do not fit into other groups. Their flowers are egg-shaped or elongated, rather than conical, but otherwise (in height and flowering time, for example) they resemble the Darwins. In some catalogues they are listed as "late spring-flowering tulips" or are included with the Darwins; others feature them as a sub-category within one or other of these groups.

Among the Cottage hybrids, 'Halcro' has long oval carmine-red flowers and is good for windy sites; 'Mrs John T. Scheepers' is considered to be the best yellow tulip ever produced; 'Princess Margaret Rose' has yellow flowers with a broad red irregular edge to the magnificent petals; and 'Smiling Queen', rosy pink paling to a silvery pink at the edges of the petals, stays in flower longer than most of the other varieties.

HALCRO

MRS JOHN T. SCHEEPERS

PRINCESS MARGARET ROSE

Tulips of long ago
Cottage tulips were already becoming less common in Victorian times. In 1895 a writer in a magazine named THE GARDEN observed that "We all remember the sweet-scented old cottage-garden Tulips of years ago; but, alas! how rarely do we see them now-a-days."

39

BALLADE

Lily-flowered tulips

The petal shape of these elegant flowers is completely different from that of the tulips most widely grown. Instead of being blunt and rounded, the petals are long, somewhat narrow, and pointed with reflexing tips; when half open, the flower seems to have a "waist." The whole plant is graceful and slender, though it retains the vigour of the Darwins, with which the other parent, *T. reflexa*, was crossed more than a century ago. Using these varieties, it is

WEST POINT

possible to create a different atmosphere and impact than that normally obtained with tulips.

'Marilyn' is white with featherings and markings of rose-red; 'Ballade' has white-edged dull-purple petals of an unusual shade; 'Ballerina' is a deep true orange, with particularly pointed petals and a bonus in the form of fragrance; 'West Point' is an outstandingly pointed flower, an intense true yellow and very reflexed; 'White Triumphator' is a candidate for the white border with a faint green streak on the outside of each petal. The height is generally 20-24in (50-60cm).

WHITE TRIUMPHATOR

40

Fringed tulips

The tulips in this new category are somewhat similar to parrot-flowered tulips (see page 45) in that their petal edges are cut and jagged. They are neat-flowered plants and the tips of their petals sport a spiky fringe – but there is no curling or deep cutting of the entire margin of the petals as there is with the parrots. They are pretty and unusual, and as yet there are not many of them.

'Canova' is an unusual lavender colour, intensified to a deeper purple in the centre of the petals; 'Fancy Frills', 21in (52cm), is aptly named, its flowers being a delightful rose-pink with a broad white triangular section on the outside of each petal; 'Maja', 28in (70cm), is light yellow; 'Red Wing', 18in (45cm), true scarlet with a black base; 'Warbler', 20in (50cm), is a deep golden-yellow and has the most deeply cut fringe.

CANOVA

FANCY FRILLS

WARBLER

Turkish "lilies"
In 1548 French traveller Pierre Belon wrote that red lilies were found in every Turkish garden. It seems likely that these were tulips since the Turks favoured varieties with pointed lily-like petals.

41

ARTIST

Viridiflora tulips

Another new class comprises the viridiflora tulips, which are becoming increasingly popular, especially with flower arrangers. They are characterized not by green flowers but by a green band of varying length and breadth on the outside of each petal. They are tulips you either love or hate – some people feel the basic colour is ruined by the green band, but it undoubtedly lends them a curious orchid-like quality that is definitely exotic.

One of the most popular viridiflora hybrids is 'Artist', 10in (25cm), which has rose-apricot as the main colour, a broad green band on the outside from the base to the tip of the petal, and twisted pointed petals into the bargain. 'Esperanto', 10in (25cm), has the bonus of white edges to its broad leaves and a deep rose-pink as its base colour. 'Florosa', 20in (50cm), is a deep rose-pink colour on the top half of its petals, which are edged with white; the rest of the petal is yellowish cream, with a broad central band of green. 'Hummingbird', 14in (35cm), is golden-yellow and green in almost equal proportions. 'Spring Green', a strong grower that reaches 18in (45cm), has white, cream, and yellow as its base colours, the lower half of the flower being green.

FLOROSA

SPRING GREEN

42

Rembrandt tulips

Although Rembrandts are officially classified as a distinct group, in catalogues they are not normally listed separately. They are, in fact, forms of Darwin or Cottage tulips, or of another old class called Breeder tulips, that have been infected with a virus by aphids, which carry the disease from plant to plant as they feed.

The virus causes an attractive "breaking" of the main colour, so that it seems to be feathered and striped. This phenomenon has existed since the early days of the garden tulip – and it was greatly admired, as can be seen from the Dutch flower paintings of the seventeenth century, many of which featured Rembrandt tulips in the foreground.

Rembrandt (1606-69)
The great Dutch painter of the seventeenth century, whose name is given to Rembrandt tulips. Many growers offer varieties (see below & next page) with "broken" colouring reminiscent of the tulips that appear in Dutch flower paintings.

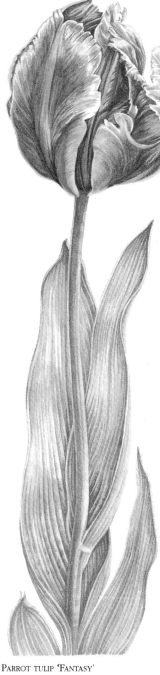

PARROT TULIP 'FANTASY'

Breeder tulips

Although no longer classified separately, these handsome tulips were an interesting group, as the colouring of their single oval flowers leaned towards browns, bronzes, and sombre purples. They have a special significance in that Dutch growers thought they were the tulips most likely to break, i.e. produce streaked and flamed flowers in their progeny, when used in breeding.

Tracking down true "broken" tulips is not easy, since Cottage tulips are not always listed separately and Breeder tulips no longer exist as a class. Moreover, so much hybridizing has occurred that most of them have vanished. However, it is still possible to find what were once called "florist's tulips" in private collections, and they can be seen at the *Hortus Bulborum*, a tulip museum and garden at Limmen in Holland.

There are also certain varieties, both among the groups described already and those to follow, that are reminiscent of the "broken" tulips. Notable examples include 'American Flag', which has dark-red markings on a white base; the peony-flowered 'Carnaval de Nice', 16in (40cm), which is white flamed with red; 'Cordell Hull', cherry-red on white; 'Flaming Parrot', 28in (70cm), yellow flamed with scarlet; 'Gay Presto', 26in (65cm), flamed and feathered red on white; 'Golden Brocade', a brownish red feathered with yellow and bronze; 'Insulinde', with violet markings on yellow; and 'Montgomery', white edged with deep red. 'Golden Brocade' and 'Insulinde' may be seen in private collections, as might the very rare 'Black Boy', which has black markings on chocolate brown. Average height where not mentioned is 24in (60cm).

FLAMING PARROT

Parrot hybrids

Like lily-flowered and fringed tulips, parrot hybrids depart from the standard petal shape. They have single flowers and are sometimes sports of Darwin tulips, although some of them may have been derived from *T. gesneriana dracontia*. Thanks to successive hybridizations of the garden forms, parrot tulips have become a distinct group, characterized by petals with much crested, almost frilly, deeply cut edges.

The original kinds grown in the seventeenth century had stems that were not strong enough to support the large, heavy heads adequately. Consequently, in old paintings and botanical illustrations they are nearly always seen with twisted stems. However, breeding has now produced a strain of strong-stemmed parrot varieties, capable of holding their heads up even after heavy rain. For the most part, their height is 20-22in (50-55cm).

'Flaming Parrot' and 'Gay Presto' are described opposite; 'Fantasy' is a pretty parrot, deep and light pink with occasional streaks of green; 'Black Parrot' is, as its name suggests, virtually black in colour; 'Estella Rynveld' is delightful, flamed with strawberry- red on white; 'Orange Favourite' has pink tints in its deep orange base colour, and green feathering on the outside of the petals.

ESTELLA RYNVELD

ORANGE FAVOURITE

45

ANGÉLIQUE

Double late tulips

Also known as peony-flowered tulips, these are possibly a sport of *T. gesneriana* and have rounded petals that curve inwards – in contrast to "early doubles," which have pointed, lightly reflexing petals, making them look more like double waterlilies. Modern peony-flowered varieties have been bred to have stout stems – especially necessary with such heavy double flowers. Height is around 16-20in (40-50cm).

'Angélique' is a beautiful pure-pink colour, with a yellow-and-cream base; 'Carnaval de Nice' has already been described (see page 44); 'Lilac Perfection' is the colour of its name, paling to white in the centre; 'Mount Tacoma' is a superb snow-white flower that stands up well to rain and gales.

Multiflora hybrids

Also flowering late in the season, but as yet lacking an official category of their own, are the relatively new multiflora hybrids. These carry several flowerheads to one stem, a characteristic derived mainly from such species as *T. biflora*, (a small white-and-yellow tulip from the Caspian and Caucasus regions with up to five heads); *T. aucheriana* from Syria (pink with a yellow-brown basal blotch and one to three heads); *T. celsiana* from Spain (yellow with red outer flushing and one or two heads); and *T. polychroma* from Iran (white-and-yellow, with up to five heads).

Attractive garden multifloras include 'Georgette', which has yellow flowers finely edged with red and feathered on the outside with the same colour; 'Happy Family', a deep pink shading to light pink on the margins; and 'Orange Bouquet', which is light red with a yellow base. All three are about 18-20in (45-50cm) tall.

MOUNT TACOMA

HAPPY FAMILY

46

SPECIES TULIPS

BEFORE DISCUSSING CLEARLY IDENTIFIED SPECIES, mention should be made of *T. gesneriana*, even though it is not listed as such in bulb catalogues. Nevertheless, it is immensely important, as it is thought to be the parent of all garden tulips and is the collective name given to the tulips introduced to Europe, from 1554 onwards, from Turkey. Generally the flowers are 2-4in (5-10cm) long and have pointed petals with a dark blotch at the base. Height is 12-18in (30-45cm), flowering time mid to late spring. The colour of the blooms is variable; but most are red, although white and yellow strains occur too.

TULIPS, 1798
Robert John Thornton
from THE TEMPLE OF FLORA

47

T. TURKESTANICA

T. CLUSIANA

T. CLUSIANA CHRYSANTHA

Early-flowering species

Besides *T. fosteriana* and
T. kaufmanniana (see pages
32-3), one early-flowering species
that is particularly decorative,
and also interesting to grow, is
T. turkestanica. The small creamy-
white flowers, which are starlike
and have a yellow blotch, appear
in late winter or early spring on
stems 8in (20cm) tall. What makes
T. turkestanica such a delight
to grow is the fact that it can
produce as many as nine flowers
on one stem. Larger-flowered than
T. biflora, it is better value for
the garden, especially as it flowers
so early in the year – though
to do so it has to have a warm,
sheltered position.

Midseason species

The midseason species include
a very famous one, *T. clusiana*,
nicknamed the "lady tulip." This
delicate and graceful species
was grown by Clusius in the sixteenth century. Found in Iran,
Afghanistan, and Kashmir, it has
pointed narrow petals that open
to a starry shape. The flowers are
white on the inside with a purple
basal blotch, but the outermost
petals are rose-red on the outside.
As a result, when they are half
open they appear to be striped.
The height is about 12in (30cm).
T. clusiana chrysantha is now
considered to be a variety of this
species, although still often listed
as *T. chrysantha* in catalogues. A
brilliant yellow, it makes a striking
plant for rock gardens.

   If you are looking for a tulip to
naturalize in a sunny spot, the
Greek species *T. hageri* spreads
well of its own accord and is an
attractive and unusual flower. The
three outer petals have a central
outer band of green edged with
deep red; the inside is a deep
brownish red with a deep-green
basal blotch, and the broad petals

narrow suddenly to a point.
Height is about 6in (15cm), and
there is an offshoot, 'Splendens',
that is multi-flowered.

T. praestans is an unashamedly
brilliant red with no basal blotch,
and is also multi-flowered, having
up to four heads to a stem 8in
(20cm) tall. A strong-growing
species from Central Asia, it is a
good tulip for rock gardens. The
variety 'Fusilier' is slightly taller
and even more outstanding, with
orange-scarlet flowers. There is an
interesting offshoot from the
species, *T. praestans* 'Unicum',
that has a wide band of yellow
edging the leaves (the flower is
the same colour as the parent).

T. urumiensis is a low-growing
multi-flowered species from the
northwest of Iran, with a stem
only 6in (15cm) or so tall emerg-
ing from a rosette of leaves. The
golden-yellow flowers have olive-
green bands on the outside of
the petals and are starlike when
fully open. There are three to five
flowers on each stem.

T. PRAESTANS 'FUSILIER'

T. PRAESTANS 'UNICUM'

T. sylvestris
*The only true European tulip is a
pretty buttercup-yellow. It grows in
dry or grassy places and spreads
by underground creeping stems.
It has one or two large, sometimes
fragrant, flowers to each of its
15in (38cm) stems and prefers a
confined, sunny position.*

T. URUMIENSIS

49

T. LINIFOLIA

T. BATALINII

T. TARDA

Late-flowering species

Unlike the garden tulips, not many of the species tulips that are described in this book flower late in the season. However, by way of compensation, there is an immense range of late-flowering garden tulips to choose from.

T. linifolia, a native of the area around Bukhara in Turkey, is scarlet with a deep-purple blotch. *T. batalinii* is so similar to it that some authorities regard it as an albino variety, and certainly it has the narrow leaves of its reputed parent; the flower colouring is creamy yellow with a deep-yellow or pale-olive basal blotch. Both kinds are about 6in (15cm) high.

T. celsiana, from Spain and the North African region, is part of the same group as *T. sylvestris* but flowers towards the end of mid spring or in the late spring. Starry and bright yellow when open, it presents a reddish appearance when closed. It carries its fragrant flowers on 6in (15cm) stems, sometimes two or three at a time. Both these species do well in rock gardens that get plenty of sun.

Another possibility for a sunny rock garden is *T. marjolettii* from the French Savoy. Although often included with the species tulips in catalogues, this is probably not a true species but simply a descendant of the *T. gesneriana* group (see page 47). Its basic colour is a very pale yellow that changes to white as it matures, but it is flushed purplish-red on the outside. Its height may be as much as 18in (45cm).

T. tarda, a species native to Turkestan, flowers readily and is particularly eye-catching as it has starry yellow flowers liberally tipped with white. The narrow leaves tend to lie on the ground. Each 6in (15cm) stem may carry six flowers, so a few bulbs can provide a considerable display.

CHAPTER

III

CARE AND CULTIVATION

SHED NO TEARS! O SHED NO TEARS!
THE FLOWER WILL BLOOM ANOTHER YEAR.
WEEP NO MORE! O WEEP NO MORE!
YOUNG BUDS SLEEP IN THE ROOT'S WHITE CORE.

FROM "FAERY SONG"
JOHN KEATS 1795-1821

Commercial tulip cultivation
*The Dutch bulb industry supplies
markets all over the world with cut
flowers and bulbs for planting. The
famous tulip fields of Holland are
a magnificent sight in springtime.*

52

Buying bulbs

The time to plant tulips is mid autumn or early in late autumn. The earlier date is best for the early spring-flowering species and their varieties. The bulbs are therefore offered for sale in garden shops and garden centres towards the end of the summer and early in the autumn.

If you want to order them from specialist suppliers, the new season's catalogues are usually available in midsummer. Ordering from catalogues adds mail costs to the prices; nevertheless, they offer a much better choice of varieties, and many of them are illustrated with superb colour photographs, so you can see what the flowers are like. Beware, though – such catalogues are extremely tempting!

If you are buying bulbs from a local shop or garden centre, look for ones that have a circumference of about $4^{1}/_{2}$in (11cm). Any that are smaller will not give good results – except for species bulbs, which can be $2^{1}/_{2}$-$3^{1}/_{2}$in (7-9cm). Have a good look at the bulb to make sure that it is not soft or misshapen, or marred by disease spots, blotches, or other defects. The base should be firm, there should be a crisp brown skin, and there should not be any visible sign of a new shoot.

Be wary of advertisements offering collections of bulbs, unless from reputable suppliers. Some-times large numbers of bulbs are sold at enticingly low prices. However, very often the bulbs are small and they may even be diseased (with eelworm, for instance, though that may not be immediately obvious). Flowers from such bulbs will be small or non-existent, so it is advisable to buy collections from specialist suppliers.

One of the best ways of choosing tulips is to see them at a flower show or growing in a show garden. This will enable you to compare the flower size and height of different varieties and will also help to remind you their flowering time.

Tulips in the garden

Tulips are extremely versatile flowers for spring and early-summer displays. As indicated by the guide to flowering times (page 29), a succession of species and varieties can provide colour for about fourteen weeks. Most varieties remain in flower for about ten days to three weeks, depending on the temperature. The cooler it is, the longer the flowers last.

At one time tulips were almost invariably grown in rows, perhaps with low-growing plants between them – and beds full of tulips planted in this way can provide an eye-catching and gloriously colourful sight.

However, such an arrangement doesn't suit the smaller-flowered or shorter species tulips. They need to be enjoyed individually and planted in small groups of two or three, or perhaps half a dozen at the most, preferably on rock gardens or in rock borders. The wild tulips found in Turkey, Greece, Iran, and other countries in the same regions, frequently grow in dry rocky places, sprouting from between boulders, out of gravel, and from steep rocky banks, as well as being found in open fields and on grassy slopes.

Delicately elegant, these small species combine well with other small bulbs flowering at the same time, such as chionodoxa, scilla, grape hyacinths (*Muscari*), and the blue, pink, and white flowers of *Anemone blanda*. Like tulips, all of these prefer well-drained rocky soil and will die down as summer approaches, enabling you to plant annuals above the bulbs.

Tulips also look good planted alongside paving, flights of steps, and paths with hard surfaces. Their own formality goes well with the precise lines of stonework or brickwork, and the subdued colouring of the stone or brick complements the brilliance of the flowers. On patios, they are ideal for inserting in gaps between paving slabs. The appearance of paths can be enhanced and softened by planting a row of tulips on each side; and flights of steps look spectacular with a pot brimming with tulips standing on each step.

Formal bedding is an outstanding way of displaying the magnificence of the large-flowered varieties. It was much favoured in the nineteenth century, and the patterns achieved were miracles of colour-blending and cultivation. Tulips can look stunning grown in a bed by themselves, relying on variety of flower, leaf colour, height, and form (lily-flowered, parrot, double, etc.) to create a spectacular and extremely attractive effect.

Alternatively, they can be part of a mixed bedding scheme. For instance, you can use forget-me-nots to form an underplanting beneath the pink-flowered 'Elizabeth Arden', or below the rose-pink and white 'Valentine' or pale-pink 'Queen Bartigon'.

Tulips and wallflowers can make a dazzling combination, especially if red, orange, yellow, and bronze flower colours are used – such as the tulips 'Golden Apeldoorn' (golden-yellow), 'Temple of Beauty' (lily-flowered, orange), and 'Lanseadel's Supreme' (a splendid red), together with mixed or brilliant single-colour wallflowers such as 'Orange Bedder' and 'Fire King'. Aubrieta, pansies, violas, primroses and polyanthus, violets, and double daisies can also be used to provide a pleasing contrast to tulips planted as a main bedding display.

Another handy, if less common, use for tulips is to disguise the bare ankles of roses in the spring – bringing a splash of colour that is particularly welcome in a formal rose garden at that time of year.

Layered gardening
Some gardeners go in for layered gardening, with different plants providing a series of "tiers" from the ground up. With a scheme of this kind, tulips can be used for the tier above the ground cover. For instance, the pink-and-white 'Fancy Frills' makes a charming colour combination grown through the velvety silver-grey foliage of "lamb's ears" (Stachys byzantina). Such layered gardening is suitable for mixed or herbaceous borders and island beds.

55

Soil preparation

Tulips do not require a rich soil, but they do need good drainage. A heavy soil, such as clay, that holds moisture even in dry weather makes the bulbs susceptible to infection by soil-borne fungus diseases, resulting in rotting and death. A low-lying position with a high water table has the same effect.

If your soil is a clay type, you will therefore need to improve the drainage in order to provide the right conditions for tulips. Preferably a few weeks before planting, mix in two or three handfuls of coarse sand (not builders' sand) or grit per square yard/metre. Also, add a layer 1in (2.5cm) thick – or more if available – of sphagnum peat, leaf mould, cocofiber, composted bark, or similar material.

The best soil for tulips is sandy – and also fairly deep, since ideally advance digging should be to a depth of about 16in (40cm). However, such soils (and the same applies to stony or gravelly ones) are usually undernourished and need the addition of a granular fertilizer as well as some form of organic matter. A slow-acting balanced organic or inorganic fertilizer is best for this purpose. In order to help retention of the fertilizer, mix in peat or other bulky organic materials, such as those mentioned above, too. However, don't use rotted farm manure or garden compost unless the preparation is done some months before planting (in early or mid summer, for example), so there is time for the manure or compost to be fully assimilated.

A good time to prepare a site for tulips is early autumn, after the first rain has come, as the soil is easy to work then. If deep digging to two spades' depth is too arduous or time-consuming, single digging to one spade's depth is possible. However, tulips planted at this shallower depth produce smaller offsets (though more of them) and do not live as long as those planted more deeply. While digging, remove all weeds and large stones, and mix in any sand, fertilizer, or organic matter thoroughly and evenly.

56

Deep digging

The best way to improve drainage and fertility is turn the soil over to two spades' depth, then fork well and dig in sand & organic matter.

*1 **Dig a trench** about one spade deep and 3ft (90cm) wide. Remove the soil to the other end of the plot (so you can fill the last trench).*
*2 **Divide the trench in half** lengthways, then dig out the first half another spade deep to create a stepped bottom.*
*3 **Fork in sand/organic matter** in the bottom of the deeper half.*
*4 **Return the soil** dug out in Step 2 to the deeper half of the trench.*
*5 **Dig a new trench** alongside the first one, about 18in (45cm) wide and one spade deep. Use the soil from it to fill the first trench.*
*6 **Continue digging trenches** in this way across the plot. Use the soil removed from the first trench to fill the last one*

3 Fork in sand/organic matter

4 Return the removed soil

1 Dig a trench one spade deep

5 Dig a new trench alongside

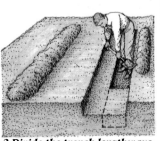

2 Divide the trench lengthways

6 Continue across the plot

57

Planting & spacing

THE BIGGER THE BULB IS, THE DEEPER IT SHOULD BE PLANTED, the average depth needed being 6in (15cm) – which means digging a hole 8in (20cm) deep. Bulbs planted at this relatively shallow depth produce a larger number of offsets. Although these take longer to mature to flowering size, the bulbs are less liable to rot if the soil is heavy. Another advantage is that they are easier to dig up once the flowers have faded if you are planning to plant a summer-flowering display in their place.

The planting depth for the smaller species bulbs need only be 3-4in (7.5-10cm), but bulbs with a circumference larger than about 5in (12cm) are better planted at a depth of 10-12in (25-30cm). This may sound excessive – but when they are growing in the wild tulips are capable of pulling themselves down to surprising depths. Moreover, deep planting enables you to put bedding plants above the bulbs as they die down. Bedding plants, being tempo-rary, tend to root shallowly, which allows the tulips to ripen undisturbed. Finally, deep planting is one way of ensuring that the bulbs will not be eaten by mice!

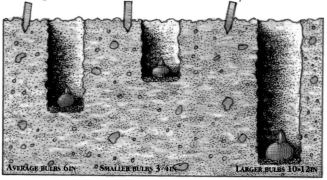

AVERAGE BULBS 6in   SMALLER BULBS 3-4in   LARGER BULBS 10-12in

PLANTING DEPTHS FOR TULIP BULBS

Spacing for most garden varieties should be about 8in (20cm), but the smaller species tulips can be planted more closely, about 4in (10cm) apart. A little sand sprin-kled at the bottom of the planting hole will help improve drainage. Plant the bulb firmly on the bottom of the hole, flat side down, then fill in the soil firmly around it. Mark the spot with a label, taking care not to pierce the bulb with the marker.

AFTERCARE

FOR PEOPLE WHO DO NOT HAVE a great deal of time for gardening, one of the great advantages of growing tulips is that you don't have to do much to them once you have planted the bulbs. In the first year, early in the spring, apply a dressing of a balanced fertilizer (preferably with more phosphate than nitrogen or potassium) at half the normal rate. In succeeding years, apply a similar dressing at the normal rate to ensure that your tulips continue to flower well. Keep the ground free of weeds.

Deadheading
Unless seed is required, deadhead as soon as the flowers have faded.

Bulb planters
To make bulb planting faster and easier, use a planting tool that cuts and lifts a plug of soil from the ground. Some models drop the plug of soil back into the hole when you squeeze the handle.

LIFTING & STORING

IT IS NOT ABSOLUTELY ESSENTIAL to dig up tulips every year. So long as they are in a position that suits them, with good drainage and plenty of sun, they will flower and increase quite satisfactorily year after year. They will of course become crowded in the end, then their quality will diminish and you will need to dig them up and sort them.

Before doing so, let them die down completely, so the leaves can feed the new bulbs. The main new bulb will flower the following year, and one of the offsets may do so as well (see pages 30-1).

Flower initiation occurs as early as mid spring; and flower formation for the next season develops from this during the summer and is completed by mid autumn. If you have to dig up tulips before the leaves have died, replant the bulbs in a shady place immediately so they can finish maturing. Then about the end of early summer or in mid summer, they can be dug up for storage.

Before storing bulbs, clean off the soil. Also, remove the old withering roots and the remains of the leaves and old bulb scales. Cut the flower stem down, leaving about 2in (5cm), or pull it away gently if it is loose. Choose the largest of the offsets and store them in single layers in trays, out of sunlight, in a cool well-ventilated building until planting time.

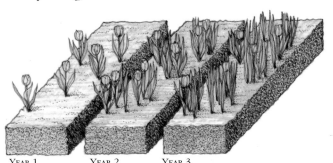

YEAR 1   YEAR 2   YEAR 3

LEFT UNDISTURBED, TULIPS WILL INCREASE YEAR AFTER YEAR

INCREASING & FORCING

Planting offsets

Enlarging a stock of tulips is simplicity itself if you use the offsets produced naturally every year. The smaller ones can be planted about 3in (7.5cm) deep and left in place until they flower – some two to four years later, depending on their size at planting. The largest of the off-sets should flower the following year, provided that it has a circumference of at least 4in (10cm).

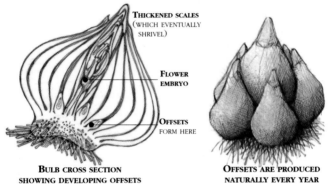

THICKENED SCALES
(WHICH EVENTUALLY
SHRIVEL)

FLOWER
EMBRYO

OFFSETS
FORM HERE

**BULB CROSS SECTION
SHOWING DEVELOPING OFFSETS**

**OFFSETS ARE PRODUCED
NATURALLY EVERY YEAR**

Tulips from seeds

Alternatively, you can sow the seeds, either as soon as they are ripe or in late winter, in sandy compost in a cold frame outdoors. Germination should take place in early or mid spring. Plant out the resulting seedlings in their flowering positions $1\frac{1}{2}$-2 years after sowing. They will flower $2\frac{1}{2}$-$3\frac{1}{2}$ years later.

Forcing

Plant tulips for forcing in a container 6in (15cm) in diameter in early autumn, with the nose of each bulb just above the surface of the compost. The bulbs should not be touching, and a container of this size is large enough for about six. Water well and place the container in complete darkness in a temperature of 40°F (4°C) for about twelve weeks. Keep the compost just moist. Then move the bulbs into the warmth – about 65°F (18°C) – but continue to keep them without light until the stems have grown another 2in (5cm). Then put them in a dimly lit place and gradually introduce them to normal daylight.

Tulip Troubles

IF TULIPS ARE GIVEN WELL-DRAINED SOIL AND A SUNNY PLACE in which to grow, they will generally remain healthy – but even so, there are a few troubles that can afflict them and these are described below.

Mice

These are one of the biggest problems, as they eat newly planted bulbs. To deter mice, plant deeply or spray the soil with a harmless repellent and put holly leaves in the planting holes.

Tulip fire (BOTRYTIS TULIPAE)

The symptoms are small yellow spots on the leaves, stems that wither as they emerge from the soil, buds covered in a grey furry mould, and flowers with brown or white blisters. Infected bulbs have yellow or brown patches. Dig up and destroy as soon as seen, and spray the top growth of the rest of your tulips with a fungicide that is specifically recommended for the purpose. If tulip fire has appeared during the season, soak surviving bulbs in a solution of the same fungicide before you store them.

Tulip eelworm

Symptoms are stunted plants, ragged leaves, discoloured flowers bent over to one side, and pale streaks and cracks in the stems. Bulbs that have been attacked are soft at the base, light in weight, and feel dry. Inside, they are discoloured and look greyish. Destroy bulbs that have been attacked by eelworm, and do not plant tulips in that part of your garden for at least ten years.

Grey bulb rot
(RHIZOCTONIA TULIPARUM)

When tulips are attacked by this disease, new shoots either fail to appear or are brown and rotting when they do. Internally, the bulbs becomes pinkish or greyish. Unfortunately, there is no cure. It is therefore necessary to remove affected bulbs, including those that have sprouted, and burn them. Also, remove the soil below and around them. Replace with fresh soil from elsewhere, and refrain from growing tulips in that area of your garden for at least five years.

Blindness

The buds emerge – but they are withered and yellowish white, and are borne on stems only 1in (2.5cm) or so high. This can be due to high temperature while they are being transported from the grower or during storage in the summer. Blindness can also be caused by digging up bulbs too soon or removing the leaves immediately after flowering.

Virus disease

As mentioned previously, this is the cause of "breaking" in tulips' flower colouring, whereby a plain colour has streaks and patches of a different colour. The disease is carried by aphids (greenfly and blackfly) and can spread rapidly. All infected bulbs should therefore be destroyed as soon as signs of the disease appear, or at least replanted at a distance from uninfected ones.

CONTAINER GROWING

Tulips are ideal for container cultivation and a boon for frustrated gardeners without a garden in which to grow plants. Balconies, windowsills, verandahs, basement areas, and flat roofs are all suitable places, especially if they are in a sunny, south-facing position.

Tulips in containers also look good in gardens and, being portable, are particularly useful if you want a summer display to take their place. Once the flowers start to die, the containers can be removed and the new bulbs left in the compost to finish maturing, so there is no need to dig them up. Patios and terraces, front doors and other entrances, stairways and poolsides are all possible sites for containers outdoors.

With the revival of interest in terracotta containers, many delightful designs are now available – including French and Italian Renaissance styles and reproductions of classical Greek or Roman urns, all of which help to create a warm Mediterranean atmosphere. Besides these, there are wooden troughs and tubs, half-barrels, reconstituted stone planters, strawberry barrels, etc. The selection is vast. The only essential criterion, horticulturally speaking, is that the container should be deep enough, as tulips generally need 3in (7.5cm) of compost beneath them and at least 4in (10cm) on top.

When planting a container, use a good proprietary compost. Make sure there are drainage holes in the bottom and provide a shallow layer of drainage material about ½in (1.5cm) thick. Space the bulbs 5in (12.5cm) apart for garden varieties, 2in (5cm) for the smaller species tulips. Once you have planted the container, keep it in a cool, dark place until the spring. Keep the compost moist, without letting it get soggy; if they do not have sufficient moisture, the bulbs will not grow. In early spring (late winter for species tulips), move the container to its flowering position.

BIBLIOGRAPHY

Many books and journals have been consulted,
and the following will be found to make useful and pleasurable reading:

The Book of Tulips Tom Lodewijk, Macmillan (USA)/Cassell 1979
Bulbs Roger Phillips & Martin Rix, Pan Books 1989
Classification List & International Register of Tulip Names
Royal General Bulbgrowers' Association, Hillegom, Holland 1987
Collins Guide to Bulbs Patrick M. Synge, Collins 1961
Flowers and their Histories Alice M. Coats, A. & C. Black 1956
The Genus Tulipa Sir A. Daniel Hall, Royal Horticultural Society 1940
Great Gardens of America ed. Carroll C. Alkins, Coward-McCann 1969
An Illustrated History of Gardening A. J. Huxley,
Royal Horticultural Society/Paddington Press 1978
Tulipomania Wilfred Blunt, Penguin Books 1950
Tulips Z. P. Botsehantseva (ed/trans. H. Q. Varekamp), Balkena 1982
Tulips and Daffodils John C. Mather, Collingridge 1961
The Year-Round Bulb Garden Brian Matthew, Souvenir Press 1986

ACKNOWLEDGEMENTS

The producers gratefully acknowledge the following individuals,
organizations, and sources that have assisted in the
creation of this book.

For the supply of photographs and pictorial material we are grateful to:
Christopher Blom of Walter Blom & Son Limited,
Bulbgrowers, Seedsmen, & Nurserymen, Watford, Hertfordshire, U.K.
Annet Brouwer of the International Bloembollen Center,
Hillegom, The Netherlands.
KAVB Library, Hillegom, The Netherlands.
Pat Brindley, Horticultural Picture Library,
Cheltenham, Gloucestershire, U.K.
Shirley Curzon.